Edith Blake

Exploring Poetry Forms

Wider Perspectives Publishing ¤ Hampton Roads, Va. ¤ 2022

All writings herein are property of Edith Blake and are her own creations, all rights reserved to author. Wider Perspectives Publishing reserves 1st run of printing rights, but all materials revert to property of the author at time of delivery. All rights to republication of items inside thereafter revert to the author and she may parcel items to contests and anthologies at will. No reproduction of this book, in part or whole, may occur without the permission of the author.

The poem *Fire Dancers* was previously published in Skipping Stones, 2006

Copyright © Edith Blake, May 2022, Portsmouth, Va.
Wider Perspectives Publishing, Hampton Roads, Virginia
ISBN: 978-1-952773-57-0

contents

Form		Page
	Trimeric	1
	Tricube	3
	Cinquain	4
	Alphabet	5
	Anagrammatic	6
	Tautogram	7
	Clerihew	8
	Emotion	9
	Diamonte	11
	Diminishing	12
	Windspark	13
	Kimo	17
	Dodoitsu	18

contents ctd...

Form	Page
Waka	19
Haiku	20
Tanka	22
Gogyohka	23
Nonet	24
List	25
Freeform	30
Ekphrastic	35
Bio	Rear Cover

Exploring Poetry Forms

Trimeric

This form has four stanzas with the following format: First stanza is four lines and the others have three lines and then each following stanza starts with the corresponding line for the first stanza. (example second stanza starts with the second line of the first stanza)

The Cardinal

I am always with you
Your guardian angel
Protecting and watching over you
As you go about living

Your guardian angel
The cardinal you see daily
Flying by your window

Protecting and watching over you
At times directing your thoughts
Giving strength to go on

As you go about living
Doing daily task
And enjoying life

Blake

The Butterfly

Majestic in your flight
As you flitter across the meadow
Going from blade of grass to flower
Spreading your wings to fly again

As you flitter across the meadow
Your colors blend with your surroundings
Creating a beautiful sighting

Going from blade of grass to flower
As you make your way around
Blending in at times

Spreading your wings to fly again
On to another flower or bud
As you move about your realm

Tricube

This is a three stanzas poem with each stanza containing three lines with each line having three syllables.

Unity

Understand
that we all
need to be

United
in accord
against evils

That divide
causing hate
and not love

Peace

Calm quiet time
Enjoying
Reading book

Relaxing
Mood setting
Atmosphere

Tranquil trance
Inspiring
Awesomeness

Cinquain

This is a five line poem comprised of 2 syllables in the first line, 4 syllables in second line, 6 syllables in third, 8 syllables in fourth, and 2 syllables in fifth.

Garden

Flowers
Gardenia, rose
Violets, sunflowers
Brighten area around house
Smell great

Rose

Yellow
Beautiful rose
Velvety smooth glossy pleasant
Eye pleasing great smelling feel soft
Wonder

Alphabet

This poem form is written using each letter of the alphabet in the poem.

Zebra

The stripped zebra who had additional colors of brown and white, ran from the danger of the lion managing to not yield to being killed, valiantly emerging quickly with a joyful inspiring unique look only to see a Xerus being captured.

Xerus

The Xerus ran quickly across the desert escaping from being captured by zagging wildly and jauntily under the bushes and growing mindful of his surroundings increasing likelihood of keeping a plentiful nut variety for the year.

Writer

Writer sat quietly gathering thoughts before setting pen to paper kindling sparks hopefully ideas came together managing amazing creativity instead of jumbled nothingness unfortunately, little developed enough for outstanding verse and rhyme yielding zilch and much x-ing out.

Anagrammatic

This poetry form you pick a word and write a poem using only words you can spell from the word.

Word equality

Quietly ate quail
Yet yeti tail quite equal
Lite ale yea, tea aye

Word Baluster

I
True blue seal ate rat a bear sat at bus

II
Slate blue beast let bat rest as last seat

III
Star luster rates real best blast

IV
Let us eat bear lest bear eats us

V
Late sale last seat at rates a real steal

Tautogram

This poem is written using only words that start with the same letter.

Cat

I
Curiosity caught creative cat catching, creeping, chasing, clamoring, cross carpet causing chaos.

II
Catnip clown creating castrophic consequences captured cat's concentration centering cozy calming concept.

III
Courageous cat curiously capsized canoe crossing creek.

Tomcat

The terrific tomcat thought twice thus terminating the thunderstorms, though topsy turvey thoughts teased through time to turn things thunderous therefore turning tomcat to tiger, terrifying the tribe.

Blossoms

Beautiful blossoms bright
Big bold becoming bountiful
Bluebells backed by babbling brook
Befitting blooms, birds, bucks, bees, bushes
Brimming breath

Blake

Clerihew

This form is a four line poem with four lines with an AABB rhyme scheme.

The cat batted at
The tiny rat
Playing catch
With the paper batch

Emotion

This poetry is used to describe emotions using descriptive language with 6 lines with the following form: First line state emotion, second line describe emotion as a color, third line when the emotion happens, fourth line how the emotion sounds, fifth line how the emotion smells, and sixth you restate the emotion.

Sadness
Black like the night
Happening at times of loss
Sounding like the blues
With no sense of smell
Sadness

Happiness
Bright like a vibrant red rose
Occurring at times of great joy
Sounding like the final fireworks
Smells like a beautiful floral display
Happiness

Sweetness
White as new fallen snow
Enjoying the beauty in nature
Sounds of a purring kitten
Smells like fresh baked pie
Sweetness

Blake

Anger
Red like a matador's cape
Happening when injustice occurs
People speaking out for those in need
Smelling like rotten fruit
Anger

Diamante

Diamond shaped with seven lines with the following pattern. First line 1 noun, second line 2 adjectives, third line 3 participles, fourth line 4 nouns, fifth line 3 participles, sixth line 2 adjectives, seventh line 1 noun.

Joy
Glad happy
Delighting exultating charming
Feel fortune ecstasy pleasure
Satisfying pleasing gratifying
Merry jubilant
Joy

Baby
Soft cuddly
Crawling, standing, stumbling
Toddler child infant minor
Trusting accepting relying
Gentle amicable
Baby

Cat
Black white
Running, sleeping, playing
Cheetah, tiger, lion, panther
Romping, eating, cleaning
Swift fast
Cat

Diminishing

This form you pick a word in the first line, second line you remove the first letter of the last word in first line, and third line you remove the first letter of the last word in the second line.

A passenger pointed out the shark
Sending up a loud hark
To board the ark

The cook made a start
To create a tart
But ended as art

There was only a chair
With a lot of hair
That blew in the air

Exploring Poetry Forms

Windspark

A five-line poem with the following pattern: first line "I dreamed ____", second line "I was <u>something or someone</u>", third line states where, fourth line shows an action, fifth line describes how.

I dreamed of sleeping
I am a bear
Deep in the mountains
Hibernating for the winter
In my snug warm cave

I dreamed of riding
I am a hobo
Aboard a train
Going nowhere in particular
In the wild west

I dreamed of watching
I am a spy
For an international art dealer
Looking for a valuable painting
In the local art community

I dreamed of flittering
I am a butterfly
All regal and majestic
Floating upon the wind
In a beautiful flower garden

Blake

I dreamed of climbing
I was a climber
In the mountains
Sensing the awesomeness
Watching the sunset over the trees

I dreamed of streaking
I was falling star
In the night sky
Moving across the starry sky
All bright and shiny for all to see

I dreamed of reading
I was an avid reader
In the quiet mountain cabin
Trying to solve the mystery
Before reaching the solution

I dreamed of drinking
I was wine taster
At the local winery
Looking for the perfect wine
To share with family and friends

I dreamed of forming
I was the beginning of the world
In a marvelous universe
Being created by God
In his divine love

I dreamed of roaring
I was a lion
Running free
Through the desert sand
Quietly stalking my prey

I dreamed of driving
I was a motorcycle rider
Cruising the mountains
Viewing the beautiful scenery
Through amazing lens

I dreamed of blooming
I was a summer flower
In a stately garden
Being carefully cared for
By a beautiful lady

I dreamed of sleeping
I was a calico cat
In a comfy bed
Dreaming of chasing my prey
Only to wake up and lose it

I dreamed of running
I was a panther
In the forest of great trees
Seeking my next meal
Stalking the delicious prey

Blake

I dreamed of soaring
I was an eagle
In the great blue sky
Drifting on the wind
With my wings spread wide

I dreamed of swimming
I was a porpoise
In the deep blue sea
Playing with others
As the tour boat passed

Kimo

This Israeli poetry form has 3 lines with no rhymes with the following: first line 10 syllables, second line 7 syllables, and third line 6 syllables. It was inspired by Haiku, but in Hebrew there was a need for more syllables.

Seashore

Water rushing upon the white sandy beach
Where children watched the waves
Rushing back into sea

Nature

Trees, flowers, butterflies, birds, snakes, fish, bears
Beautiful sights to adore
Colorful displays seen

Blake

Dodoitsu

This Japanese four line poem contains 7 syllables in the first three lines and five syllables in the last.

When a poet writes a poem
Expressing thoughts or feelings
Choosing carefully each word
Secrets revealing

Waka

This is also a five-line poem with a 5, 7, 5, 7, 7 syllable structure. The first two lines should make up one piece, the third and fourth line should be a second piece, with the fifth line standing on its own or a part of the second piece.

Lovers

Beautiful blossoms
Become bountiful big bed
Upon which lovers
Seal their undivided souls
Devotion to each other

Blake

Haiku

This is a three line poem with the 5, 7, 5 syllables.

Sunrise

Beautiful sunrise
Horizon bright with color
Red, pink, and orange

Sunset

Amazing sunset
Sky bright red, orange, yellow
Shining through the clouds

Fall

Cooler weather now
Trees with reds, oranges, yellow
Amazing picture

Fan

Rotating stirring
Circulating the fresh air
Providing relief

Exploring Poetry Forms

Change

Adapting new ways
Being bold to venture out
Trying something new

Black Eyed Susan

Bright sunshine blossom
Brown and yellow make you bright
Flowers of beauty

Tanka

This poetry form is a five line poem with 5, 7, 5, 7, 7 syllables or as a five line poem with 3 short lines (2,4,5) and 2 very short lines (1,3).

Paradise

What is paradise?
Is it truly a grand place?
Or something not real?
Is it beauty or ugly?
What you see defines your life.

Fireworks

We sat and watched
The fireworks of all colors
Red, blue, green, white, gold
Bursting in clear air lighting sky
Final display breathtaking

Summer Days

Lazing in the sun
By the beautiful deep lake
Enjoying the sounds
Children splashing and playing
While their parents watched with care

Gogyohka

This Japanese form is comprised of five lines with one phrase per line.

Park

Swings and slides
For children's play
Climbing and swinging
Up and down, they go
Enjoying the fun

Nonet

This form is a nine line poem starting with 9 syllables in the first line and each line decreases by one syllable till the last line is only one syllable.

<u>Football Game</u>

Boisterous crowd became roaring mob
After their team scored the touchdown
With one second on the clock
Tying the game again
Yelling go defense
Cheering louder
Going wild
Go team
Go

<u>Storm</u>

The thunderous storm raged on outside
Caused the dog to tremble in fear
While the sweet cat lay in peace
Children hide their faces
Parents assured them
All shall be well
Fear thou not
God is
Here

List

This form is a list of things, whether names, places, actions, thoughts, images, etc.

Things we Miss

So many things we miss because of the pandemic
People we love
Gathering together for fellowship
Hugging those we care for and love
Socializing with friends
Enjoying a meal out with others
Worshipping in person
Meeting together to encourage one another
Wishing things were somewhat normal again
Celebrating special occasions with friends and family
Visiting those in hospital or long-term care
Consoling friends and family when a love one dies
I hope and pray that someday we can do all these things again.

Pandemic Reflections

What has this year of pandemic taught us?
Are we any better as a person or country?
Do we show more empathy for our fellow man?
Can we follow simple rules to keep us safe?
How has it affected your way of thinking?
Are you coming out of this stronger or weaker?
Are we more aware of the way we see things?
Has it made you more aware of your need for human contact?
How have you reached out to help those less fortunate?
What has changed in you during the past year?
How do you react to the violence around you?
How has this past year made you a better person?

Blake

Garden Walk

Strolling among the flowers and trees
            What do we see?
Flowers of all different shapes and colors
            Beautiful red and pink Roses
Brilliant yellow Daffodil
            Colorful orange Marigolds
Small elegant Pansies of all colors
            Petals of white and yellow Daisies
Brown and yellow Black-Eyes Susan
            White Queen's Anne Lace
Sounds and sights we hear and see
            Chirping birds
Rustling leaves as squirrels scamper by
            Splashing water as fish jump
Croaking frogs
            Cackling geese
Buzzing bees
            Silent statutes standing around
White, marble, copper and metal
            Man, animals, birds, and such
Boats on the lake fishing and touring
            Family and friends enjoying sights
Paths we walk
            Concrete, mulch, and bricks
Wonderful smells in the air
            Fragrant flowers and herbs abound
What wonders we see
            Strolling among the flowers and trees

Pour Out

Pour out your blessings
          Showering us with gifts
Pour out your spirit
          Giving us understanding
Pour out your forgiveness
          Granting us mercy
Pour out your love
          Showing us grace
Pour out your words
          Showing us the way
Pour out your hope
          Filling us with joy
Pour out your light
          Opening our eyes
Pour out your fullness
          Releasing our burdens
Pour out your direction
          Guiding our lives
Pour out your wisdom
          Enlightening our minds
Pour out your power
          Strengthening our will
Pour out your joyfulness
          Lifting our spirit
Pour out your peace
          Quieting our hearts

Blake

Clichés

Whatever happened to these phrases?
Waste not want not
It's ancient history
Wait till your dad gets home
Stick and stones will break my bones but names will never hurt
No skin off my back
I'm warning you
What's it to you?
The quick brown fox jump over the lazy brown dog
Got to see it to believe
Ask what you can do for your country not what your country
        can do for you
Uncle Sam wants you
Silence is golden
What's wrong with you?
Blood is thicker than water
When it rains its pours
An apple a day keeps the doctor away
You will be sorry

Affirmations

I will not settle for less
I know my potential
I can do anything I set my mind to
Confident in my abilities
Willing to accept that change needs to happen
Follow the desires of my heart

True Friends

What joy a pet can bring
From those gone to those here
Angel the white wonder
Fluffy the Angora cat
Peaches the hunter of rabbits
Corkie the garden lover
Lucky the roving wanderer
Tina the yapping Chihuahua
Lady the dainty one
Tippy the white poodle
Ginger the sweet, tempered Pit Bull
Daisy the moocher
Muffy the black knight
Kelly the black Labrador
Lucy the Beagle friend
Wiggins the Tuxedo cat
Toby the Schipperke full of energy and pep
BJ the lovable cat playful and true
Archie the wiener dog what more can you say
Coco the other wiener dog
Benny the fun, loving Calico
The four wonders of Roup Street
Nigel the black sneak
Tigger the tabby
Rascal the gray ghost
Dilly the crazy silly stripped one

Blake

Free Form

This form has no set formula or style with rhyming optional. Totally up to author.

<u>Equality</u>

Why do we treat those who are different, differently?
Your sex, color, gender, social standing, or orientation, or gender
        should make no difference.
We need to look at the person from the inside out, not outside in.
Once you get to know someone who is different you gain a new
        perspective of them and yourself.
You see they are no different than you.
They have the same physical structure as you.
Equality means treating everybody fairly, using the same standards.
Just because someone has less than you, doesn't mean
        they are any different.
Life experiences make a difference in how we look at things
But those events should not affect our view of people
        who are different.
We must love one another.

<u>Listen</u>

In the silence we listen for your calling
Shutting out the noises around us
Listening to hear your words for us
Being open to your calling
Willing to do your biding
Speak to us Lord as we listen
Help us to still our busyness to hear your still small voice

America Strong Together

Pulling together for the common good
Uniting as one against this virus
We will overcome
Facing a stronger faith as Americans
Trusting in God for answers
Knowing He will calm our fears
Providing guidance to our leaders
Sustaining workers on the front lines
Giving understanding to those working on ways to a cure
Helping us see our need to get back to trust in God
Knowing He is the author of our lives
Showing us how to reach out to those in need
Caring for our neighbors young and old

Senseless Violence

What has it come to in America?
The senseless takeover of the capital by extremist trying
        to disrupt government.
Five people dead in the process, for what purpose.
All because one person cannot accept his defeat.
The results have been verified and certified to be correct.
Grow up and quit making such a fuss.
Thank you, Twitter, Facebook, and all others
        who have frozen accounts to stop his nonsense.
We need to find our way back to God and end
        this senseless violence.
We need to follow God's leading and not those
        who would do us harm.

Blake

Trust

Trust in the Lord
He will see you through
For love never fails
As we act justly, love mercy and walk humbly
Listening for his voice
Opening ourselves to his calling
Knowing he will equip you for your task ahead
Keeping our eyes on the goal
We trust in the Lord

Racism – Why?

Why is it that some people believe they are superior to others?
We are all one in God's eyes.
Just because we are of different colors does not mean
        we cannot work together.
All lives matter for we are wonderfully made by the same God.
Each individual has unique gifts and talents to use
        to make this a better world.
Just because someone is different does not make them a bad person.
All people know someone who leaves a bad taste in our mouths.
We need to start working together to stop profiling others.
How would you feel if you were considered bad because
        of who you are or what you look like?
You probably would not like it, so why do you do it to others?
Let us put aside our prejudices and work together.
For when we work together, we unite in a common cause,
        being one in God.
Finally let us remember the words of Galatians 3:28, "There is
neither Jew or Greek, slave or free, male or female,
        for you are all one in Christ Jesus."*
Work for justice for all.

                                      * New International Version

America's Disobedience – But Hope Is Alive

Why can't you obey orders that are for your safety?
How can you not be concerned for the elderly?
What does your disregard for others say about you?
Where are your morals?
Did your parents not bring you up to know the difference
            between right and wrong?
How come you won't take this virus seriously?
Are you afraid and don't know how to act responsively?
Are you so eager to get back to gathering when it is still unsafe?
Is it because you refuse to accept the new normal?
If we but rely on God, He will see us through,
Yes, social distancing, wearing masks, limiting people
        who can gather, and doing without are hard things,
        but think of those who are vulnerable before
        letting your guard down.
Let us all stop thinking about self and think about our neighbors.
Be content with the way things are until it is safe to return
        to a new normal.
Listen to those who realize the danger we face,
        and value their judgment and wisdom for
        what it means to you, friends, and family.
When we all pull together and face this crisis, we will
        make it through and be stronger for it.
Let us once again turn our hearts and minds to God and listen
        for the still, small voice of reason and let it prevail
        in your life.

Flabbergasted

How do you explain your whatchamacallit or your thingamajig?
What shenanigans have you been up to?
I am flabbergasted and bamboozled by your malarkey.
Exactly what is your whatnot and doohickey?
All of this is gobbledygook and poppycock leave me discombobulated.

Poppycock

Stop being so pernickety and get things done
Lollygagging will not get your whatsit in place
Being a whippersnapper will not help accomplished your goal
Skedaddle before you are gob smacked in the brouhaha
Being flummoxed may end having you called a nincompoop

Ekphrastic

Ekphrastic poetry is writing as inspired by another piece of art.

Meditation Room

Quiet surroundings
        Filled with sounds of trickling water
Set our minds free as we sense
        Your wonder and awe
The majesty of your glory and power
        Amongst the bread and wine

Glittering stars a blaze
        Reflecting a rainbow of colors
Crown of thorns
        Reflecting your humility
Single rose within barren branches
        Reflecting your beauty
Baby Jesus in a manager
        Reflecting your humble birth

Colors of cloth reveals your life
        Brown lowly birth
        Blue sadness
        Red blood
        Black death
        Purple majesty

Promises of your covenant and forgiveness
        Brings us to our journey's end

Fire Dancers*

Motion poetry
Flames spinning round and round
Intertwining fire

Do you count the beat?
Blending movement unison
Body flame as one

Do you feel the heat?
Burning...safe...burning again
Magic movement now

Turning spinning speed
Gentle graceful careful be...
Error unforgiven

Moving to and fro
Circling side to side circling
Behind and in front

Hear the swoosh, swoosh, swoosh
Flashing fireball spiraling
Rhyme and rhythm flow

Illusions, mystic
Visions, butterflies in flight...
Then all silent dark

Survivor

Game of outwitting, outplaying, and outlasting
Players giving it their all
Challenges meant to test their skills and strength
Team against team
Alliances important but also deadly
Figuring who to vote out
Do you take out a weak or strong player?
Immunity is the goal
Merge occurs and takes contest to another level
Now it is player against player
Immunity still the goal
Contest now make player think who and when to put someone on the jury
Ultimately a jury of those voted out decides the winner
Who will be the winner of winners and win the two million?

Grand Oak

Giant oak standing as a sentry
Guarding the creek's bank
Rope dangling from limbs
Inviting children to play
Stand hiding in the limbs
Teasing those brave enough to climb
Grab rope to swing to and fro
Releasing grip to land in creek
Splash water rush to shore
Creating waves of joy

Blake

Stained Glass

Sun rays illuminate your panes
           So, illuminate our lives

Show us your prisms of color
           Lighting our ways

Reds, blues, yellows, greens
           Life, death, resurrection

Love flowing
           Gracing abounding

Peace, joy, comfort
           Radiate in your panes

Exploring Poetry Forms

Blake

colophon

Brought to you by Wider Perspectives Publishing, care of James Wilson, with the mission of advancing the poetry and creative community of Hampton Roads, Virginia.
This page used to have many cute and poetic expressions, but the sheer number of quality artists deserving mention has superseded the need to art. This has become some serious business; please check out how *They art...*

Nick Marickovich
Grey Hues
Madeline Garcia
Chichi Iwuorie
Symay Rhodes
Tanya Cunningham (Scientific Eve)
Terra Leigh
Raymond M. Simmons
Samantha Borders-Shoemaker
Taz Weysweete'
Jade Leonard
Darean Polk
Bobby K. (The Poor Man's Poet)
J. Scott Wilson (TEECH!)
Charles Wilson
Gloria Darlene Mann
Neil Spirtas
Jorge Mendez & JT Williams
Sarah Eileen Williams
Stephanie Diana (Noftz)
Shanya – Lady S.
Jason Brown (Drk Mtr)
Ken Sutton
Crickyt J. Expression
Se'Mon-Michelle Rosser

Lisa M. Kendrick
Cassandra IsFree
Nich (Nicholis Williams)
Samantha Geovjian Clarke
Natalie Morison-Uzzle
Gus Woodward II
Patsy Bickerstaff
Jack Cassada
Dezz
Catherine TL Hodges
Kent Knowlton
Linda Spence-Howard
Tony Broadway
Zach Crowe
Mark Willoughby
Martina Champion
... and others to come soon.

the Hampton Roads
    Artistic Collective
    (757 Perspectives) &
The Poet's Domain
are all WPP literary journals in cooperation with Scientific Eve or Live Wire Press

Check for those artists on FaceBook, Instagram, the Virginia Poetry Online channel on YouTube, and other social media.

www.ingramcontent.com/pod-product-compliance
Lightning Source LLC
Chambersburg PA
CBHW021001090426
42736CB00010B/1419